wil

DOMESTIC DOGS

BASSET HOUNDS

by Susan H. Gray

SOUTHERN OKLAHOMA Library System
Ardmore, Oklahoma

The Child's World

Published in the United States of America by The Child's World®
PO Box 326 • Chanhassen, MN 55317-0326
800-599-READ • www.childsworld.com

PHOTO CREDITS
© Andrew Fox/Corbis: 9
© BrandXPictures/Alamy: cover, 1
© Daniel Dempster Photography/Alamy: 23, 27
© Ernest A. Janes/Bruce Coleman USA: 17
© Mark Raycroft/Minden Pictures: 11
© NDisc/Alamy: 21
© Norm Dettlaff/Associated Press: 29
© Penny C. Frederiksen: 19
© Petra Wegner/Alamy: 13
© PhotoStockFile/Alamy: 15
© Ron Kimball/Ron Kimball Stock: 25

ACKNOWLEDGMENTS

The Child's World®: Mary Berendes, Publishing Director;
Katherine Stevenson, Editor

Content Advisers: Barbara Brandt, Corresponding Secretary, Basset Hound Club
of America; Carol Hunt, *Tally-Ho* Editor, Basset Hound Club of America; and Randy
Frederiksen, President, Basset Hound Club of America

The Design Lab: Kathleen Petelinsek, Design and Page Production

LIBRARY OF CONGRESS CATALOGING-IN-PUBLICATION DATA

Gray, Susan Heinrichs.
  Basset hounds / by Susan H. Gray.
     p. cm. — (Domestic dogs)
  Includes bibliographical references and index.
  ISBN 1-59296-771-X (library bound : alk. paper)
  1. Basset hound—Juvenile literature. I. Title. II. Series.
  SF429.B2G73 2007
  636.753'6—dc22   2006022634

Table of Contents

NAME That DOG!

What sad-faced dog makes people laugh? What dog can follow a **scent** for miles—but cannot find its way back home? What dog has puppies that look like old dogs? What dog slobbers a lot but is still a **popular** pet? There's only one answer—the basset hound!

5

Dogs from France

Basset hounds came from France. Hunters in France had them more than 400 years ago. They used the bassets to track rabbits and other small animals.

The dogs had short legs and short hair. They were good at running through thick grass. Their fur did not get stuck on branches or weeds. They did not run fast. Hunters on foot could keep up with them. Bassets also had wonderful noses. They could follow a rabbit's scent for miles.

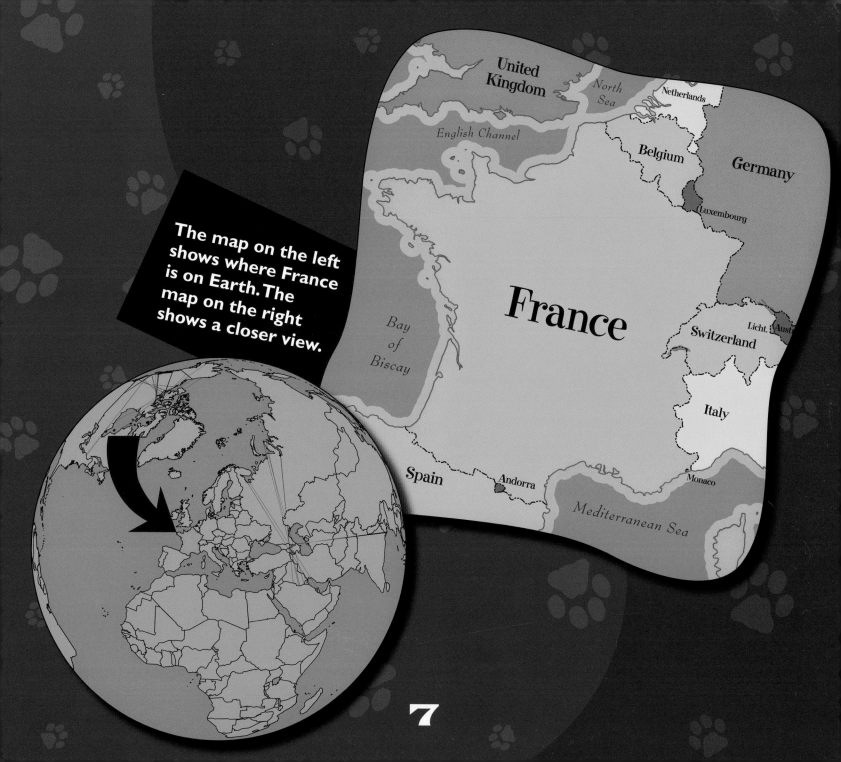

The map on the left shows where France is on Earth. The map on the right shows a closer view.

United Kingdom

North Sea

Netherlands

English Channel

Belgium

Germany

Luxembourg

France

Bay of Biscay

Switzerland

Licht. Aust.

Italy

Spain

Andorra

Monaco

Mediterranean Sea

From France, basset hounds spread to other countries. In the mid-1800s, they were brought to England. Within 30 years, many English people had bassets. Even the queen owned bassets.

Soon, people in North America found out about the basset. They liked its short, thick body. They liked its sad-looking face. And they liked its hunting skills.

Americans started entering their bassets in dog shows. In 1928, a magazine had a story about one show. It was a big show in New York. The magazine's cover showed a basset puppy. Suddenly, more people wanted basset hounds. Today, they are a very popular **breed**.

The word "basset" comes from the French word bas (BAH). Bas means "low." Bassets are very low to the ground!

These basset hounds are sitting quietly at a dog show.

Saggy, Baggy Dogs

Basset hounds are heavy dogs with short legs. They have large heads and big, deep chests. They are about 14 inches (36 centimeters) tall at the shoulder. Adult dogs weigh about 50 to 60 pounds (23 to 27 kilograms). That is about as heavy as a second grader.

Bassets have short hair, and they shed a lot. Most bassets have black, brown, and white patches. Very light brown patches are sometimes called "lemon colored."

This basset is a tricolor. It has three colors: black, white, and brown.

All dogs have skin flaps on the sides of their mouths. These flaps are called **flews**. Basset hounds have floppy flews!

Bassets' skin is loose. It is very baggy on their faces. Bassets have long, floppy cheeks and saggy necks. Their eyelids hang down over their big brown or black eyes. Basset puppies are so wrinkled, they look like old dogs.

People love bassets' faces. Some people say that bassets look gloomy or sad. It's the baggy skin that makes them look that way.

Bassets are known for their long, soft ears. Some bassets' ears almost touch the ground. They get dirty easily. Sometimes bassets run through mud puddles or dirt. Their ears pick up all sorts of muck.

Some bassets have very small patches of black or brown fur. This is called "ticking."

This basset isn't sad, but its saggy eyes make it look that way.

13

Noise, Drool, and Lots of Love

Basset hounds are friendly dogs. They like to live with families. They get along well with children. Most bassets are good with other pets.

Bassets can learn to listen to their owners. They can learn to follow **commands** and do tricks. But they can be stubborn, too! They do not do tricks just to please their owners. They do things when they feel like doing them.

This basset hound is breathing hard after playing in the park.

15

A hound is a dog that tracks or chases other animals. Some hounds follow the animal's smell. Others chase animals they see.

Basset owners must live with one messy problem. Their dogs drool—a lot! They drool when they are happy. They drool when they are nervous or upset. They drool when they are hungry. When they shake their heads, drool flies everywhere! Most owners just get used to this.

Like other hounds, bassets have their own special bark. They make a "woh-woh-woh" sound. It is deep, loud, and long.

Bassets also love to follow interesting smells. When they pick up a scent, they often forget everything else. They forget to stay in the yard. They forget to stay in the neighborhood. They simply must follow that smell! Basset owners must keep their dogs from running loose. Some bassets will follow a scent much too far. They get lost and cannot find their way back home.

Woh-woh-woh! This basset is barking at the photographer.

Basset Babies

Mother bassets often have about eight puppies in a **litter**. Sometimes they have as many as 14 or 15.

When they are born, basset puppies are round and fat. Their eyes are closed, and they are helpless. But they still look like basset hounds. They have big heads and short legs. They have loose skin, too.

These basset puppies are only one day old. They are drinking their mother's milk.

As the puppies grow, they start to look like their parents. After a few weeks, their faces get wrinkly. Their ears almost touch the ground. Their short legs can barely hold up their long bodies.

Like all puppies, baby bassets are full of energy. They love to run around. They love to **explore** new places. But they need to be **protected**. They should not run up and down stairs. They should not jump down from chairs or couches. Their short legs have to hold up big, growing bodies. Even a little jump can hurt their legs.

Bassets can live a long time. Most live to be about 10 to 12 years old. Some even live to be 17.

These puppies are about six weeks old. They are tired from playing all day!

Bassets at Work

Some people use bassets for hunting rabbits and deer. But many people keep them just as pets. Bassets are friendly to people of all ages. They are good just to have around the house.

Some people put their bassets in dog shows. They show off their good-looking dogs. They show how well their dogs behave. The best-looking, best-behaved dogs win prizes.

BEST
OF
WINNERS

MAJOR

SOUTHERN INDIANA
KENNEL CLUB, INC.

SATURDAY
MAY 29, 2004

OTOS BY...
ENNAH

Bassets that go to dog shows learn to stand a special way. They hold their heads high and point their tails. This dog's owner is helping him.

A few bassets have become actors. Bassets named Dog, Flash, and Sammy have been on TV. A basset named Fred starred in a movie. Other bassets have made commercials.

Many people enjoy tracking with their bassets. This sport tests the dogs' sense of smell. Some people even put their bassets in tracking **contests**. Before the contest, a person lays down a track. The tracklayer walks through a big field. The tracklayer makes turns and walks through short grass and tall weeds. The tracklayer drops things like gloves and scarves. Then the tracklayer leaves.

A few hours later, the contest begins. A basset is let loose in the field. Judges watch to see if the dog follows the tracklayer's scent. Several dogs are tested. The best tracker wins!

A basset's long ears help it to hunt. As the dog runs, its floppy ears stir up the air. This helps the basset pick up scents.

What do you think this basset is tracking? A person? A rabbit?

25

Caring for a Basset

Most owners say that bassets are easy to care for. Like all dogs, bassets sometimes have problems. Their big, floppy ears need extra care. When the dogs are outside, their ears pick up dirt and bugs. They get caked with mud. Owners should clean the ears at least once a week.

Some bassets get too heavy. They sit around inside all day. They eat too much and do not exercise. They get lazy and put on weight.

Bassets can often jump over low objects. This basset is jumping over bars her owner set up.

Some cities hold a "Doo Dah Parade" every year. Hundreds of bassets and their owners march in the parade. These parades raise money for basset hounds that need homes.

Basset hounds need to run and play. They love to go outdoors. Their owners need to take them for walks. They need to let the dogs run around in the yard.

Sometimes bassets get leg or back problems. These problems are caused by the dogs' short legs and long bodies. Their backbones have to **support** a lot of weight. The backbones can slip out of place. They can rub against each other. This is very painful for the dog. Sometimes bassets' elbows and knees hurt, too. This is often true of dogs that are too heavy.

But most bassets do not have these problems. They live long, happy lives! Basset hounds bring love and joy to their families.

Does this basset look as if she is smiling? She was very curious about the photographer taking her picture.

Glossary

breed (BREED) A breed is a certain type of an animal. There are many breeds of dogs, including basset hounds.

commands (kuh-MANDZ) Commands are orders to do certain things. Basset owners can teach their dogs to follow commands.

contests (KON-tests) Contests are meets where people or animals try to win by being the best. Some basset owners enter their dogs in tracking contests.

explore (ik-SPLOR) To explore is to look into something or learn about it. Puppies like to explore the places around them.

flews (FLOOZ) Flews are the flaps of skin along a dog's mouth. A basset hound's flews are very floppy.

litter (LIH-tur) A litter is a group of babies born to one animal at the same time. Basset litters often have about eight puppies.

popular (PAH-pyuh-lur) Something that is popular is liked by lots of people. Bassets are popular dogs.

protected (pruh-TEK-tud) To be protected is to be kept safe. Puppies need to be protected.

scent (SENT) A scent is a smell. Basset hounds love to follow the scent of rabbits.

support (suh-PORT) To support something is to hold it up. Bassets' legs and backbones have to support their long bodies.

To Find Out More

Books to Read

Collins, Ellen. *A Biography: My Life As a Basset Hound (By Katie the Blue Heeler)*. Baltimore, MD: PublishAmerica, 2005.

Loggia, Wendy. *Woof! My New Best Friend*. New York, Bantam Skylark, 2001.

Mars, Julie. *Basset Hounds*. Kansas City, MO: Andrews and McMeel, 1997.

Places to Contact

American Kennel Club (AKC) Headquarters
260 Madison Ave, New York, NY 10016
Telephone: 212-696-8200

On the Web

Visit our Web site for lots of links about basset hounds:

http://www.childsworld.com/links

Note to Parents, Teachers, and Librarians: We routinely check our Web links to make sure they're safe, active sites—so encourage your readers to check them out!

Index

About the Author

Susan H. Gray has a Master's degree in zoology. She has written more than 70 science and reference books for children. She loves to garden and play the piano. Susan lives in Cabot, Arkansas, with her husband Michael and many pets.